Safari Sam's Wild Animals

Freshwater Animals

A+

Smart Apple Media

Published by Smart Apple Media, an imprint of Black Rabbit Books
P.O. Box 3263, Mankato, Minnesota 56002
www.smartapplemedia.com

Produced by David West Children's Books
6 Princeton Court, 55 Felsham Road, London SW15 1AZ

Designed and illustrated by David West

Copyright © 2014 David West Children's Books

Cataloging-in-Publication Data is available from
Library of Congress
ISBN 978-1-62588-071-0

Printed in China
CPSIA compliance information: DWCB15CP
311214

9 8 7 6 5 4 3 2 1

Safari Sam says:
I will tell you something
more about the animal.

 Learn what this animal eats.

 Where in the world is the animal found?

 Its size is revealed!

 What animal group is it—mammal, bird, reptile, amphibian, insect, or something else?

 Interesting facts.

Contents

Alligators

Alligators and their crocodile cousins are the largest reptiles living in lakes and rivers. They have a ferocious set of teeth in powerful jaws, which they use to grab hold of large animals. The unlucky victim is then dragged beneath the water to drown.

American alligator

Alligators eat fish, turtles, snakes, and small mammals. But an alligator will eat almost anything, including **carrion**, and pets.

Alligators live in freshwater rivers, lakes, swamps, and marshes of the southeastern United States and the Yangtze River valley in China.

American alligators can grow up to 12 feet (3.7 meters) long and can weigh over 500 pounds (230 kilograms). The Chinese alligator is smaller, at a length of 6.9 feet (2.1 meters).

Alligators are reptiles.

Alligators leave the food they catch to rot so that it is easier to bite off chunks. Sometimes, they take a bite and spin in the water until a chunk is torn off.

Safari Sam says:
Despite their ferocious reputation, alligators are good mothers. They defend their nest from predators and help the hatchlings to water. They protect their young for about one year.

Beavers

Beavers are famous for busily building dams and transforming rivers into lakes. Gnawing down trees with their strong teeth, they create dams with tree trunks and mud. Beavers build their home, called a lodge, in or near the water using branches and more mud.

Beaver

Beavers are **herbivores** and prefer to eat leaves, bark, twigs, roots, and water plants.

 Beavers live in North America, in parts of Europe, and in West and Central Asia.

 Beavers can grow to 4.2 feet (1.3 meters) and can weigh up to 77 pounds (35 kilograms).

 Beavers are members of the **rodent** order of mammals.

 Beavers are graceful in the water. They use their large, webbed rear feet to power themselves forward and their paddle-shaped tails as rudders to steer.

Safari Sam says:
Beavers can stay underwater for 15 minutes without surfacing. They have a set of clear eyelids that work like swimming goggles.

Ducks

Ducks are found on freshwater lakes and rivers. Diving ducks **forage** deep underwater. Dabbling ducks feed on the surface of water, on land, or as deep as they can reach by upending. A few ducks, such as mergansers, have adapted to catch and swallow large fish.

Ducks eat a variety of food such as grasses, aquatic plants, fish, insects, amphibians, worms, and **mollusks**.

Ducks can be found across most of the world except in Antarctica.

The Mandarin duck grows up to 20 inches (51 centimeters) long with a wingspan of up to 29 inches (74 centimeters).

Ducks are members of the waterfowl family of birds.

Ducks are farmed in many countries for their meat, eggs, and feathers.

Mandarin duck

Safari Sam says:
Mandarin ducks nest in holes in trees close to water.

9

Greater flamingos

Safari Sam says:
Flamingos are born gray.
Adult coloring ranges from
light pink to bright red
depending on what foods
they eat and how much they
are in the sunlight.

Flamingos

Large colonies of flamingos live all around the world wading on their long, spindly legs. They feed in the shallow water of coastal areas and lakes. Flamingos use their beaks to filter muddy water away, which leaves tasty, small animals to eat. Sometimes, flamingos stomp their webbed feet in the mud to stir up food from the bottom of the water.

The flamingo's bent bill allows it to feed on small organisms such as shrimp, tiny fish, fly larvae, and blue-green **algae**.

Flamingos can be found in southern Asia, Africa, and in South and Central America.

Flamingos grow up to 5 feet (1.5 meters) long and have a wingspan of 5 feet (1.5 meters).

Flamingos are birds.

Flamingos are very social birds. They live in huge colonies, which can have thousands of flamingos.

Frogs

In general, frogs have moist skin with large, powerful legs and webbed feet. Frogs start life as tadpoles after hatching from eggs. Gradually, tadpoles become adult frogs by losing their tails and gills, then growing front and back legs and developing lungs.

Safari Sam says:
Frogs use their sticky tongues to catch flies and other small moving prey.

Common frog

Frogs eat small animals, such as flies, snails, slugs, and worms.

Frogs can be found on every continent except Antarctica.

Common frogs have a body length of 3.5 inches (8.9 centimeters).

Frogs are amphibians. An amphibian can live in water as well as on land.

The Australian Rocket Frog can leap over 6.5 feet (2 meters). That is more than 50 times its body length of up to 2.2 inches (5.5 centimeters).

Herons

Herons are medium-to-large-sized birds with long legs and necks. They feed on a variety of water animals. The bird's most common hunting technique is to stand motionless in shallow water and wait until prey comes within range. Then, the heron spears the prey with its beak.

A heron's diet includes amphibians, fish, **crustaceans,** reptiles, mollusks, and water insects.

Herons live on all continents except Antarctica.

The largest species of heron is the Goliath heron, which stands up to 5 feet (1.5 meters) tall.

Herons are birds.

Some herons use bait, such as pieces of bread, to lure their prey within striking distance.

Boat-billed heron

Safari Sam says:
Herons are sometimes called "the patient fishermen" because they can wait a long time without moving for prey to come within range.

15

Hippos are herbivores and eat plants growing on or near the riverbank.

Hippos only live in Africa.

Hippos can weigh up to 3 tons (2.7 metric tons).

Hippos are mammals.

The word "hippopotamus" is an ancient Greek word for "river horse."

Hippopotamus

16

Hippos

The word "hippo" is short for hippopotamus. This large animal spends most of the day keeping cool in rivers or lakes. They emerge at dusk to graze on grasses that grow on land.

Safari Sam says:
When hippos bask on riverbanks, their skin produces an oily, red liquid. This liquid acts as a skin moisturizer and sunblock that also protects hippos from germs.

Otters

Otters have webbed feet and spend much of their time in the water. They make their home in a burrow near the water's edge and live in rivers, lakes, swamps, and estuaries. Otters hunt for fish, but also will eat many other water animals.

Safari Sam says:
Otters love to play and can be seen sliding down muddy banks and ending up in the water with a splash.

18

Oriental small-clawed otter

Otters feed on fish, shellfish, crabs, frogs, birds, and small rodents.

Otters can be found on most continents except Antarctica and Australia.

Some otters can grow to over 4 feet (1.2 meters) long.

Otters are mammals.

Otters can hold their breath underwater for about eight minutes.

19

Piranhas

Fish are the most common residents of freshwater habitats. One of the most well-known fish is the piranha. These fish are meat eaters and have short, powerful jaws and razor-sharp teeth.

Safari Sam says:
Piranhas have been known to attack humans wading in rivers.

Red-bellied piranha

Piranhas eat fish, insects, crustaceans, and plant matter.

Piranhas are only found in South America.

The red-bellied piranha can reach 1 foot (30 centimeters) long.

Piranhas are members of the bony fish superclass.

The black piranha has a bite that is more powerful for its size than the bite of a great white shark.

Safari Sam says:
Not all swans are white. The South American black-necked swan has a black head and neck. The Australian black swan is almost all black.

Mute swan

Swans

Swans are among the biggest of the flying birds. They spend most of their time feeding in water or in nearby fields. Baby swans are called cygnets. Sometimes they ride on their mother's back as she floats across the surface of the water.

Swans eat water vegetation and grass. They also eat small fish, frogs, worms, and mollusks.

Swans are generally found in the cooler climates on most continents except in Antarctica and Africa.

Swans can grow to over 5 feet (1.5 meters) long and have a wingspan of up to 8 feet (2.4 meters).

Members of the waterfowl family of birds, swans are closely related to geese and ducks.

Swans are an ancient symbol of love. Pairs of swans are believed to form lifelong relationships.

Glossary

algae
A simple, plantlike life form.

carrion
The flesh of dead animals.

crustacean
An animal with a segmented body that includes crabs and shrimps.

forage
To search for food.

herbivore
An animal that feeds only on plants.

mollusk
An animal that has a soft body, no bones, and usually a hard outer shell.

rodent
A mammal with front teeth that continuously grow and are kept short by gnawing.

Index